W9-BLD-222

J
636.73
MEI

13.95

Whitcomb Assoc.

10/01

DOGS SET IV

Saint Bernards

FISKE PUBLIC LIBRARY
110 RANDALL ROAD
P.O. BOX 340
WRENTHAM, MA 02093

Cari Meister
ABDO Publishing Company

visit us at
www.abdopub.com

Published by ABDO Publishing Company, 4940 Viking Drive, Suite 622, Edina, Minnesota 55435. Copyright © 2001 by Abdo Consulting Group, Inc. International copyrights reserved in all countries. No part of this book may be reproduced in any form without written permission from the publisher.

Printed in the United States.

Cover Photo: Ron Kimball Studios
Interior Photos: Ron Kimball Studios (pages 5, 7, 11, 13, 15, 17, 21), Corbis (pages 9, 19)

Editors: Bob Italia, Tamara L. Britton, Kate A. Furlong, and Christine Fournier
Art Direction: Neil Klinepier

Library of Congress Cataloging-in-Publication Data

Meister, Cari.
    Saint Bernards / Cari Meister.
        p. cm -- (Dogs, Set IV)
    Includes bibliographical references and index.
    ISBN 1-57765-474-9
    1. Saint Bernard dog--Juvenile literature. [1. Saint Bernard dog. 2. Dogs.] I. Title.

SF429.S3 M45 2001
636.73--dc21

                                                        00-045380

Contents

The Dog Family

Over thousands of years, people have trained and bred wild dogs for different uses. Some, like the Saint Bernard, were bred for work. Others were bred for companionship.

Dogs are part of a **family**, called Canidae. Dingos, jackals, wolves, and foxes are also part of the canid family. Canids have many of the same **traits**.

Dogs and wolves both have an excellent sense of smell. They sniff and find things that people cannot. In fact, dogs can smell much better than humans!

Today, millions of dogs live with families all over the world. There are more than 400 different dog breeds. Saint Bernards are one of the biggest breeds.

The Saint Bernard is a popular breed throughout the world.

Saint Bernards

Saint Bernards have a long, courageous history. Long ago, the only way to cross the Swiss Alps was through a snowy mountain pass. For most of the year, the pass was under 32 feet (10 m) of snow. People often got lost in the snow. Many people died.

Around 1,000 years ago, a **monk** named Saint Bernard built a **monastery** in the Swiss Alps. The monastery gave shelter and food to weary travelers. The monks helped rescue lost people.

By the early 1700s, the monks used huge dogs to help them find and rescue people. These dogs were later called Saint Bernards.

Saint Bernards could find and dig people out from under the deep snow. The dogs would then lick the people's faces to **revive** them. Often, the big dogs would lie down next to people to keep them warm. Saint Bernards helped rescue more than 2,000 people!

Today, a railroad runs through the Great Saint Bernard Pass. The **monastery** and its dogs are still there. But the dogs there do not rescue people anymore. Now, most Saints are devoted family pets.

The Saint Bernard can plow through deep snow.

What They're Like

Saint Bernards are **massive**, gentle, easygoing dogs. They are patient. They are also good with children. Saint Bernards are smart and loyal. And they get along great with other family pets.

Saint Bernards love to be around people. They are affectionate. They do not like to be left alone or in a **kennel** for very long.

If Saint Bernards become bored or lonely, they can get into trouble. Bored Saint Bernards may dig huge holes in the backyard or chew on furniture.

With the right training, most Saint Bernards are obedient. They like to please their owners. But some Saint Bernards can be **stubborn**.

Saint Bernards are strong. They can learn to pull small carts or wagons. In the past, Saint Bernards pulled carts of milk, cheese, and eggs to market.

Saint Bernards are patient and gentle with children.

Coat and Color

Saint Bernards can have short coats or long coats. Short coats are smooth and thick. Long coats may have some wavy hair. All Saint Bernards have thick, bushy hair on their thighs and tails.

Saint Bernards with long hair need more brushing than those with short hair. But all Saints love to be brushed. Saint Bernards should be brushed about once a day. During shedding seasons, regular brushing will cut down on the mess.

Saint Bernards have patches of brown on their coats. The brown can come in many shades. Some Saint Bernards have patches of a deep reddish brown. Others have patches of yellowish-brown. They can also have patches of **brindle**. Saint Bernards have white on their chests, tails, necks, faces, and feet.

Even short-haired Saint Bernards have a warm, thick coat.

Size

Saint Bernards are a giant breed. They are tall, strong, and heavy. Male Saint Bernards stand about 28 inches (70 cm) from the shoulders. Female Saint Bernards stand about 25 inches (64 cm).

Saint Bernards are the heaviest breed. They usually weigh between 125 and 180 pounds (57-83 kg). Some Saint Bernards get even bigger.

Saint Bernards have huge heads. A Saint Bernard's head is about the size of a basketball! Saint Bernards have strong jaws and droopy mouths.

Because of their droopy mouths, Saint Bernards drool. They drool when they exercise and when they are hot. They also drool when they eat. They even drool when they are excited.

Saint Bernards have strong shoulders, necks, and legs. Even though Saint Bernards are strong, they are gentle.

The Saint Bernard is one of the biggest dog breeds.

Care

Like all dogs, Saint Bernards need to visit the **veterinarian** once a year. Veterinarians can tell you how to clean your dog's ears and trim its toenails. They also give shots that prevent diseases like **heartworm** and **rabies**.

The veterinarian will make sure your dog has a healthy life. Like many giant breeds, Saint Bernards do not live a long time. Most Saint Bernards live for eight to ten years.

Saint Bernards' feelings can be hurt easily. Make sure you scold your dog in a firm voice. But do not scream or use violence. Praise your Saint often. Give it lots of affection.

Saint Bernards cannot handle hot weather. If left outside in the summer, Saint Bernards can have **heatstroke**. Never leave your dog in a car!

Like all dogs, Saint Bernards need lots of love.

Feeding

Saint Bernards like to eat meat. Most dog foods are made from meat. They have all of the **nutrients** that Saint Bernards need. Ask a **veterinarian** or a breeder to help you choose the right dog food.

Saint puppies should be fed puppy food until they are six months old. They need to be fed three times a day. Saint Bernards grow fast, so they eat a lot. And adult Saints will eat even more.

An adult Saint will probably eat up to 2 pounds (1 kg) of dog food a day. Adult Saint Bernards should be fed twice a day. If you feed your Saint only once a day, he is more likely to get **bloat**.

Bloat is common in Saint Bernards. It is a serious disease that can kill a dog. To prevent it, do not exercise your Saint Bernard an hour before or after eating.

Always have fresh water for your Saint. Saints need lots of water, especially when it is hot outside. But do not let your Saint drink too much right after exercise. This can lead to **bloat** as well.

Because they grow so fast, Saint Bernard puppies need to be fed more often than adults.

Things They Need

Because Saint Bernards are so big, they do best in large homes. Like all dogs, Saints need a quiet place of their own. In an apartment, there may not be a quiet spot big enough for this gentle giant.

Saint Bernards do not need much exercise. One walk a day will keep a Saint Bernard healthy. In hot weather, the Saint will want to stay by the air conditioner.

Saints like to play with soft stuffed animals and plastic dog bones. Do not give your dog real bones or **rawhide** bones. Saints may swallow them whole.

Saint Bernards should be bathed about once a month. The yard or a big bathtub are good places to wash your Saint. But it may be difficult to find a place to give a 200 pound (91 kg) dog a bath!

Saint Bernards should always wear dog tags. That way, if a Saint gets lost, someone can call its owner.

Saint Bernards like to hike, especially in cool weather.

Puppies

If your Saint Bernard is going to have puppies, get ready! Make the mother a roomy **whelping** box. The box should be about 6 feet (2 m) long and 5 feet (1.5 m) wide. Put an old blanket in the box. Put the box in a quiet, dark place.

After about nine weeks, the mother will be ready to have her puppies. She will go to the whelping box. Her temperature may drop. She might not want to eat.

Saint Bernard puppies are born in little **sacs**. The mother dog will clean the sacs off the puppies. After they are clean, the puppies will find their way to their mother's **mammary glands**.

After the puppies eat, they will want to sleep. Make sure the mother does not lay on her puppies. She may accidentally trap them underneath her.

A Saint Bernard puppy usually weighs about 1 pound (.5 kg) when it is born.

Glossary

bloat: a condition in which air gets trapped in a dog's stomach, causing pain, shock, and even death.

brindle: a gray, tan, or tawny color with darker streaks or spots.

family: a group that scientists use to classify similar plants and animals. It ranks above a genus and below an order.

heartworm: a worm that usually lives in the right side of a dog's heart and causes tiredness, coughing, and even fainting.

heatstroke: a condition marked by sweating, high body temperature, and fainting. It is caused by a long exposure to high temperatures.

kennel: an animal cage or shelter.

mammary glands: the glands in female dogs that produce milk.

massive: large, bulky, and heavy.

monastery: a place where monks live.

monk: a man that lives in a monastery and spends his life serving a religious community.

nutrients: important parts of a diet that all living things need to survive.

rabies: a sickness of warm-blooded animals which causes abnormal behavior and increases saliva, often leading to death.

rawhide: untanned cattle hide.

revive: to bring back to life.

sac: a pouch within a plant or animal, often containing a liquid.

stubborn: being headstrong and not giving in.

trait: a feature of a person or animal.

veterinarian: a person with medical training who cares for animals.

whelp: to give birth.

Internet Sites

Animal Planet - Guide to Your Dog
http://animal.discovery.com/dog_guide/dog_guide.html
This site from Animal Planet has information on choosing a dog, caring for a dog, and training a dog. Use this site to find out what breed of dog is right for you.

How to Love Your Dog
http://www.howtoloveyourdog.com
Here's a site just for kids! Learn how to be your dog's best friend. Read stories, quiz your knowledge of dogs, and read some doggy riddles!

Natural History Museum Berne Switzerland
http://www.nmbe.ch/abtwt/saint_bernard.html
This is the National History Museum Berne Switzerland home page. Find out more about the famous Saint Bernard rescue dogs. Read about Barry, the most famous Saint Bernard of all time. See historical drawings from the Saint Bernard monastery.

These sites are subject to change. Go to your favorite search engine and type in Saint Bernards for more sites.

Index